Stargazing

Mark Pichora

Illuminating Books
www.MarkPichora.com

Copyright © 2017 by Mark Pichora
First edition - 2017

Words and pictures by Mark Pichora.
Some illustrations contain elements of imagery courtesy of NASA.

All rights reserved. No part of this publication, text, or illustrations may be reproduced or transmitted in any form, or by any means, electronic or mechanical, including photocopying, recording, or any information browsing, storage, or retrieval system, without written permission obtained beforehand from Mark Pichora.

ISBN
978-0-9959645-2-5 (Hardcover)
978-0-9959645-0-1 (Paperback)
978-0-9959645-1-8 (eBook)

1. JNF051040 Juvenile Nonfiction, Science & Nature, Astronomy
2. JNF042000 Juvenile Nonfiction, Poetry, General

Distributed to the trade by The Ingram Book Company

Hello, Earthling!

I'm Zap, and yes, I am an alien! Well, to me, *you're* the alien, but my mom said that Earthlings don't like it when we call them that.

You probably haven't seen an alien before, but if you look closely, you can find me in every picture of this book!

You'll also see me pop up in boxes like this whenever I have something totally amazing to tell you about space. These aren't part of the story, but I think you'll like them.

Your alien friend,

Zap

P.s. I wrote you a poem! Can you figure out what it's about?

> *When crossing the desert, or wide open seas,*
> *Wise men and sailors are lost without these;*
>
> *They're wondrous, and ancient, and endlessly vast;*
> *You look at them now, but you're seeing their past!*
>
> *Look deeper and find there is much they can teach;*
> *Of nature, and fortunes for those who beseech;*
>
> *Round they go, often, and round they are, each;*
> *And they're always around, but they're far out of reach!*

Do you know what *"they"* are? Think about it!

Enjoy the story!

In a nice little spot, quite a long way from town,
Jane watched the sun as it slowly went down.

And when every last ray disappeared from her sight,
The forest went dark, and the day became night.

"Look at the stars!" she said, "Dad!", so excited;
The sky burst to life and young Jane was delighted.

She ooh'd and she ahhh'd and she started to wonder,
What marvels were hid in the stars she stood under.

Is it true that they burn at a million degrees?
Is there life out in space? Is the moon made of cheese?

"Why, my Jane!", said her dad, as he set down his flask,
"If you wanted to know, you had only to ask.
For I know a few things, and I'm happy to tell,
And space is a place that I know very well.

"Somewhere up there, in those twinkling stars,
There's a *whole other world*, more *wondrous* than ours!"

Jane perked her ears, but she knew her dad well,
And he liked to play tricks in the stories he'd tell.
Was he making them up? Well, she never quite knew.
They could be made up... *Or they could be all true!*

"It's a beautiful planet, with great sweeping plains,
And luminous forests that glow when it rains.

It's a planet like Earth, with a tad bit more danger!
The trees there grow taller.

The creatures grow stranger!

"There are *rock-eating lions* and *human-sized ants!*
Spikeyback bears and big *bear-eating plants!*"

But Jane sensed a ruse — she said, *"Human-sized ants!*
And what kind of bear would get eaten by plants?
You're trying to trick me, Dad, that's what I think!"

But her dad simply smiled, and gave her a wink…

"A whole other world... but its oceans are cleaner! The air there is fresher. The forests are greener.

"The mountains are higher, with sharp, jagged peaks,
And waters cascading to far below creeks!

"*A whole other world*... but its sky has two moons! That rise over shimmering, turquoise lagoons."

"Two moons!", giggled Jane, "No, I think you're confused! Moons come in ones, Dad! They don't come in twos!"

"Think again, my dear Jane! They most certainly do! Moons come in *manies!* They come in twos, too. It's a beautiful place, Jane, but that's just the start; This world has people! And here's the best part…

"They're *smart*, Jane!

So smart that our brains, in their view,
Don't even seem smarter than cows seem to you!"

Well, now, Jane might be young, but she wasn't naïve,
And this was all getting too much to believe!
But she couldn't help wondering, "*What if* it were true?
A whole other world, *and aliens too!*"

"Are you sure you're not dreaming? Or making stuff up?"
And her dad nearly choked as he drank from his cup.

"So you think that I'm dreaming! Or making up lies!
'Cause I tell of a place you've not seen with your eyes.
Well, it's not just a dream, and no word of a lie!
I believe that it's *real*, and I'll tell you just why.

"There are *billions and trillions* of stars in the sky,
And most are too far to be seen with your eye.

"Why, if each little star was a fine grain of sand,
You'd have far too much sand to pick up with your hand!
You would have a great pile of such height and such girth,
You'd have more grains of sand than the beaches of Earth!

Billions and trillions? What are those??
Let's start with a million. If you were counting the seconds as they go by, it would take you about 12 days to count to one million. Counting a billion seconds would take much longer - almost 32 years! One trillion seconds? 32 *thousand* years!!

"More grains of sand than the beaches of Earth!"… *Really??*

Have you been to a beach? Have you seen all that sand? Seems crazy, right!?

Well, let's see… Your solar system is part of the *Milky Way* galaxy, which contains over 100 billion stars. But the *Milky Way* is only one galaxy of about 1 to 2 *trillion* galaxies in the universe, and there could be many more that are just too far to see!

So, if there are a trillion galaxies, and if we assume that each galaxy has about the same number of stars as the *Milky Way*, then that means there are at least a *100 billion trillion* stars in the universe!

That's 100,000,000,000,000,000,000,000 stars!

Is that more than the number of grains of sand on all of Earth's beaches? Well, let's just say that if a single teaspoon holds 40,000 grains of sand, then a 100 billion trillion grains of sand would cover Earth's entire land mass in a layer of sand more than 3 inches deep!

"But they're not grains of sand! Just look at the *Sun!*
It's the closest of stars, and it's only but one.
That's right, Jane! The Sun! It's our very own star.
And it's bigger than Earth! And it's bigger *by far!*

Mars

Earth

Mercury   Venus

"It's bigger than Earth, and it's bigger by far!"

Did you think the sun was just small, blindingly bright light in the sky?

Well it's not! It's actually very, *very* big! You could fit 1.3 *million* Earths inside of it!

In this picture, the planets and the Sun are all shrunken down so that you can see how big they are compared to each other. (They are shrunken "to scale").

The dotted lines show the path of each planet as it circles around the sun. These are called "orbits", and they are actually much, *much* bigger than shown here. Mercury should actually be 50 feet away from this book, and Neptune should be more than 11 football fields away!

"So, if each little star is a far-distant Sun,
With planets around, and 'round most, more than one,
Then with *billions* and *trillions* of stars in the sky,
The number of planets is wonderfully high!
A *staggering*, mind-blowing, *cosmic* amount!
Too many to name and too many to count!

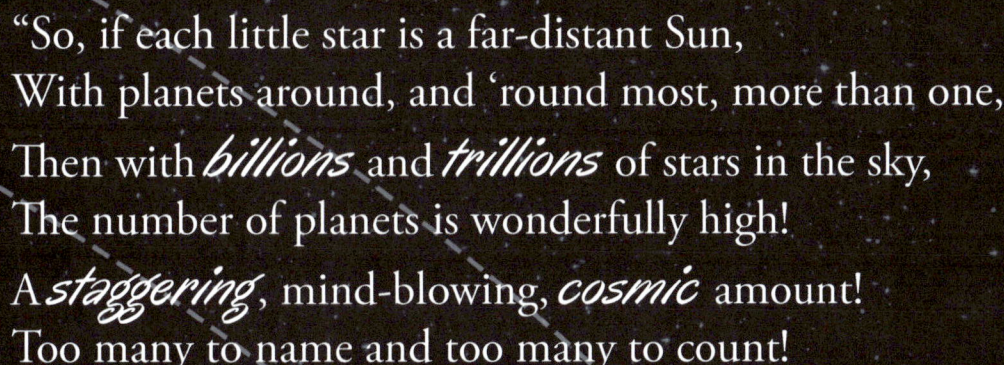

Neptune

Saturn

Jupiter

Uranus

"And if life happened here, then my dear, if you dare,
You had better believe it can happen out there —
Any one of those planets could spark up some life,
And with so many of them, the chances are *rife!*

"Of course, some are all dry,
and there's nothing to drink…

"And some are so *cold* that you'd freeze in a blink!

"Some planets are *hot*, with bright fire and flair!
And you'll run out of breath on the ones without *air*.

"If a planet's too small, you will feel much too light!"

Gravity is stronger on some planets than others. Isn't that weird?

If you weigh 100 pounds here on Earth, you would only weigh 38 pounds on Mars, and only 16 pounds on the moon. Imagine how high you could jump! On the Sun, you would weigh 2,800 pounds. You'd be squished by your own weight!

Gee, Zap, what's gravity?

Gravity is a force that attracts all objects together. There is even gravity pulling your face towards a delicious bowl of ice cream, but we usually only feel the gravity of very *massive* objects, like planets. The *heavier* the two objects are, and the *closer* they are to one another, the *stronger* the gravity between them will be.

Jupiter, Saturn, Uranus and Neptune are all much, *much* bigger than Earth, but their gravity is surprisingly weak because they're made of light, gassy materials. The four planets closest to the Sun — Mercury, Venus, Earth and Mars — generate much more gravity for their size because they're made of heavy rocks and minerals.

Zap's Solar Travel Tips

The Sun
1 star

First, let me say that the only reason I gave this place even *one* star, is that it is *actually* a star.
Extremely *sunny* and *hot* — 5 million degrees celsius on the surface, 16 million at the core. Basically all hydrogen and helium (no air!). Radioactive. Also, the gravity here is a major downer.
Verdict: Great for postcards, but do NOT go!

Mercury
0 stars

Cute little planet, but expensive! I booked for 2 days, but the days here are 120 Earth-days long. Oops! Also, the years are only 88 Earth-days, so the calendar is a mess. Hot days (ex: 400°C) and cold nights (ex: -190°C). Dress accordingly!
Verdict: Light gravity is fun, but no air. Skip it!

Venus
0 stars

After Mercury, I was glad to see that Venus actually has an atmosphere. Too bad it's almost entirely made of carbon dioxide! It's toxic and it traps heat like crazy, so it's hot here — about 500°C most of the time! Oh, and did I mention the volcanoes? They're everywhere!
Verdict: Explosive lava pit? No thanks!

Earth
5 stars!!

This place is paradise! Really, 5+ stars! My only complaint is that a certain *local species* is making a really big mess here. I won't mention any names…
Verdict: Highly recommended! Don't spoil it!

Mars
3 stars

Great place! Sure, it's cold (-60°C), and its atmosphere is a little thin (and like Venus, mostly carbon dioxide), but this place has potential. There's water here too! Rumour has it you humans want to build a station here… Cool!
Verdict: Two thumbs up!

Jupiter
2 stars

So, I came in for landing and, *surprise* — there's no land! This is a *gas planet!* Nearly triple gravity and very stormy! I canceled my booking and I'm hoping to get accomodation on one of its 67 moons. Europa sounds nice — I hear there might be life in its underground oceans!
Verdict: Skip Jupiter, but check out the moons!

Saturn
1 stars

Nearly crashed my ship in the planetary rings — and for what? It's another gas giant! At least it has moons — 62 of them! One of them (Titan) is bigger than the planet Mercury!
Verdict: Beautiful, but lacks *survivability* and other basic amenities.

Uranus
1 star

For some reason, people are always excited about Uranus. "Hey Zap", they say, "send us pictures of Uranus", or "Hey Zap! Uranus is full of stinky gas!" Anyway, it's another gas planet with lots of moons (27!). The years are long here — 84 Earth years! Icy-cool at about -200°C.
Verdict: C-c-c-c-ooooold!

Neptune
1 star

Get away from it all on Neptune! The *last* planet — 30 times farther from the Sun than Earth! The years are even longer here than on Uranus (165 Earth years!). Watch out for the big storms with 2,200km/h winds!
Verdict: Great spot for some alone time!

Now the thing about Earth, is that Earth is just right!

We have just what we need.
And we're comfortable.
Quite!

Earth, Sweet Earth!

When you think about it, you're pretty lucky that you were born on Earth. It's the only place for at least 24 trillion miles that isn't entirely deadly!

Life flourishes here because it has a very nourishing environment. Over 70% of the Earth's surface is covered by oceans, which is really important because water is essential for life. Earth also has a nice atmosphere that gives you air to breathe and helps to keep your weather in a comfortable range, while also protecting you from the harsh conditions of space. It's a safe distance from the Sun, and it receives just the right amount of sunlight to support life.

There's no place like home, Earthling!

"And a planet like ours might be quite rare to find,
But I'll bet you my hat there are more of its kind.

"I'll bet my left shoe, there's at least one or two,
And I'll bet you my right, there are more out there too!

I bet you can find them in more than one place.
I'll bet you they're scattered like marbles through space!

"I'll bet you my hat there are more of its kind!"
As wonderful as Earth is, it's really just a tiny and insignificant little speck in an unimaginably vast universe. Who knows what amazing worlds might be out there, just waiting to be found!

"I bet there are worlds where everyone's happy.
And probably some where they're grumpy and snappy.

Worlds of peace! Without hunger or greed;
Where they don't say *'I want'*, only *'what do you need?'*

Worlds with mountains of *glittering gold!*
But when everything glitters, the glitter gets old.
Can't eat it, can't drink it, no good for a bed;
So they treasure the soil and oceans instead!

"Now, there might be a world that's ravaged by war!
It was a nice place, but it's not anymore.

The folks who lived there, they just couldn't agree;
And they fought over land, and they poisoned the sea.
Now the seas are dried up, and the lands are all gray,
And the kids had to leave 'cause there's nowhere to play!

Where did they go? Well, I can't say for sure.
Most likely a planet that's wholesome and pure!

"A world where fruit hangs from every tree,
Where the sun sets at two, and it's back up at three!

"Just think of a place, my dear Jane, any place!
And there might be a place just like that out in space.
Now, we might never prove it. There's no way to tell.
But space is so big that the chances are swell!

"Where the Sun sets at two, and it's back up at three!"
Impossible? Nope! Some planets orbit around two Suns, or *more*, so it's possible for one to rise just as the other has set. Wakey, wakey!

"And that's why I say that up there, in the stars,
There's a whole other world, *more wondrous* than ours!"

"Let's go to it, Dad! Let's go explore space!
I'll bring my new boots, and some rope, just in case!
I want to see aliens! Please, can we go?"

And her Dad said, "Of course! But I think you should know,
That if all that you've got is your boots and some rope,
Then our mission to space will be quite without hope!

"Those planets aren't close! They're *fantastically far!*
It takes more than four years just to *see* the next star!

We'd need our own spaceship that's *faster than light!*
And alas, we have none — but the aliens might!

Who knows, Jane! Who knows if they've already found us!
Just watching, and listening, and *living around us.*

"It takes more than four years just to see the next star!"

Weird, right?! I mean, you can look up and see the stars any time, so how can it take 4 years to see the closest one? Well, here's the catch: you can see it now, but you're not really seeing it *now*. Confused? No problem! Let 'ol Zap explain.

First, I need to tell you about light. Light travels fast. *Very* fast. 300 *thousand* kilometers per second! (186 thousand miles per second). In the time it takes you to blink, a ray of light could travel around the entire Earth *three times!*

When sunlight reaches your eye, it has just finished a trip of 150 million kilometers that takes about 8 minutes and 20 seconds to complete. For sunlight to reach planet Neptune, at the edge of the Solar System, it takes over 4 hours.

Now, let's look deeper into space. The *nearest* star outside of your solar system is called *Proxima Centauri*. It's 4 *light-years* away, which means that it takes over 4 years for light to travel the distance from here to there. *That's* why it takes "*more than 4 years just to see the next star!*"

Imagine! If I was at Proxima Centauri right now, and I started waving to you as you were watching through a powerful telescope, you wouldn't see me wave until four years later! Incredible!

They might be disguised to look just like we do,
And for all that you know, my dear,
I am one too!"

You look at them now, but you're seeing their past!
Some stars are millions, or even *billions* of *light-years* away, so the light we see from those places has been flying through space for a really, *really* long time. That's why, when you look out into the stars, you're not just looking through space, you're also looking through time! You are seeing things as they were a long time ago. My home planet is about 160 million light years away, and when my people look at Earth these days, all they see are dinosaurs!

Now, I know what you're thinking: "if all those stars and planets are so far away, then how can we explore them??" Well, as Jane's dad says:

"We'd need our own spaceship that's faster than light!"

The problem is, scientists on Earth believe that it is impossible for anything to travel faster than light, which would mean that even the *fastest* space ship that anyone could *ever* build would still take at least 4 years to carry you to your nearest neighbouring star.

Maybe one day *you* will find a way to get there faster! Of course, I could send you my old copy of *Warp Drives, Worm Holes and Teleportation Made Easy*, but where's the fun in that?

Well, that got Jane thinking a minute or two…
It was silly, of course! It was surely not true!

But she started to fret, and her hairs went all stiff!
And she stewed and she worried and wondered, *"what if!"*

What if he's an alien! *What if* it were true!

"But, Dad!" she said, shyly,
"You're *not*, though—

Are you??"

But her dad simply smiled, and gave her a wink,
And poor little Jane didn't know what to think!

Her heart started racing! Her world was askew!
Her dad was an alien!

...And yours might be too!

The End!

Thirsty for more mind-boggling and amazing information about space?

Read on, my brilliant little Earthling!

P.s. You can stop looking for me now! I'm not hiding anymore :)

Space Q&A with Zap!

Is the Sun the biggest thing in space?

Not even close! It's an average type of star called a *Yellow Dwarf*. Many stars are much, *much* bigger than our Sun. Look at the picture on the next page and you'll see what I mean!

Will the Sun ever burn out?

It sure will! The Sun burns *hydrogen* in a process called *nuclear fusion*, where hydrogen atoms are fused into a heavier atom called helium. This process releases an amazing amount of energy!

The Sun has already been burning for about 4.5 billion years, and it has enough hydrogen left to burn for about 5 billion more, so don't worry, it will keep shining for a long, *long* time!

What happens then?

As the Sun burns up the last of its hydrogen, it will grow into a much bigger star type called a *red giant*. As it grows, it will swallow up Mercury, Venus, and (gulp!) *Earth* in the process. Eventually, the outer gasses will explode outwards, and the Sun will lose about half of its mass. Meanwhile, the core will contract and turn into a *white dwarf* star.

What is a *white dwarf* star?

A typical white dwarf star is about half as massive as the Sun is today, but all of that mass is squeezed into a space only slightly larger than Earth, so they are *extremely* dense. If you squeezed the Empire State building smaller and smaller until it was as dense as a white dwarf star, it would be so small that you could fit two of them in your fridge!

This density gives them a very strong gravitational pull. If you were standing on one, you'd be over 100 *thousand* times heavier than you are on Earth. A glass of water would weigh more than a bus!

Sometimes, when a star many times bigger than the Sun burns out, the remaining core is so massive that it collapses under its own gravity and it becomes a *black hole* — a super-dense object (even denser than a white dwarf star) with gravity so strong that even light can't escape its pull.

Twinkle, twinkle, GIANT star!

1) Mercury < Mars < Venus < Earth

2) Earth < Neptune < Uranus < Saturn < Jupiter

3) Jupiter < Proxima Centauri < Sun < Sirius

4) Sirius < Pollux < Arcturux < Aldebaran

5) Aldebaran < Antares < Betelgeuse < UY Scuti

Black holes!

Black holes are *amazing!* We can't see them because any light that goes in gets trapped forever. You wouldn't even know they were there if it weren't for their intense gravitatational pull which influences everything around.

They can bend light, and even suck it in completely if it gets too close. They grow by swallowing up cosmic gasses, dust, rocks, planets, and even stars. Some black holes have grown to become millions, or even *billions* of times more massive than our Sun. These are called *supermassive* black holes, and they are at the center of most major galaxies.

See the picture on the next page? That's a spiral galaxy made of billions of individual stars, much like your *Milky Way*. Do you see how those stars are all swirling around, almost like planets orbiting the Sun? What do you think they're spinning around?

You guessed it! They're spinning around a *supermassive* black hole! (Actually, each star orbits the center of mass of all of the other stars, *plus* the black hole, together).

The black hole at the center of the *Milky Way* is called *Sagittarius A*. It's 26 thousand light years away from Earth and has the mass of *4 million Suns!*

Also by Mark Pichora

You're Amazing!
(Starring You)

Named to *Kirkus Reviews'* Best Books of 2016!

"Louie the Lumin and his two young friends explain some of the human body's magnificent highlights in this Seussian rhyming book… a delight for reading out loud."
— *Kirkus Reviews* **(Starred Review)**

Mark Pichora is an undercover engineer turned business professional — but is anyone convinced? The truth is, he is still a camp counsellor at heart!

Dabbling in music, skiing, and elaborate treehouse-building (for the kids!), he lives very happily in Montréal, Canada, with his wonderful wife and son, Geneviève and Léo.

Thank you, readers!

I hope you enjoyed learning all about space! Please consider leaving reviews and ratings online - they are greatly appreciated! You can do this through all major retailers (Amazon, Goodreads, B&N, and Indigo), even if you got the book elsewhere or read it at the library.

Acknowledgements

Thank you to my special internal consultants, Geneviève and Léo, who are never shy to let me know what's right, what's wrong, and what's missing.

I also want to thank a few artistic inspirations. Thank you to *Aaron Griffin* and "*WLOP*", who have done the world a great service by sharing their digital art techniques on YouTube and teaching me a little bit about drawing.

Special thanks to NASA for providing surface imagery for 7 of the 8 planets in the solar system. (All but Saturn).

Author Website

www.MarkPichora.com

www.ingramcontent.com/pod-product-compliance
Lightning Source LLC
Chambersburg PA
CBHW041127300426
44113CB00002B/86